I0800872

# WonderWorks

## Decodable Reader

### Unit 9

Mc Graw Hill

# Contents

A Fun Drum Club
by Anita Monroe
illustrated by Soo Kim
1

Wake Up!
by Jacqueline Carter
illustrated by Laura Logan
9

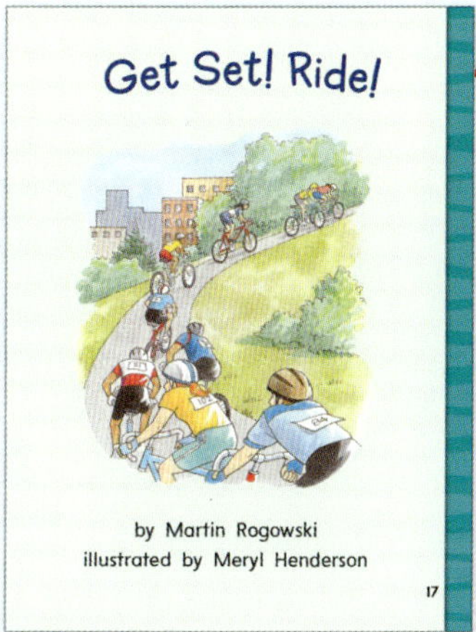
Get Set! Ride!
by Martin Rogowski
illustrated by Meryl Henderson
17

# A Fun Drum Club

by Anita Monroe

illustrated by Soo Kim

Do you **want** to hit a big drum? Bret and Greg **have** a drum club.

It is fun **here**! Grab a stick.
Hit, hit, hit!

Tap a rim and grin.
But do not crack the top.

Step up but do not trip.
Step up but do not drop
the stick.

Hit, hit, hit a drum.
Step and hit it.

Get a bus at six!

**This** drum club is fun,
fun, fun.

# Wake Up!

by Jacqueline Carter

illustrated by Laura Logan

Wake up, wake up!
Jane and Kate had a nap.

Jane and Kate gaze up.
Can they run in the sun?
It is not safe.

Kate can dig, dig, dig in.
Jane can **help** Kate dig in.
They can make a safe cave.

Jane and Kate wake up late.
The sun is not up yet.
Kate and Jane can gaze up.

Jane can see a big tan box.
Kate can see it, **too**.
Can Jane make a fun game?

Yes! Jane can hop up on it.
Hop, hop, hop on it, Kate.
Jane made up a fun game!

# Get Set! Ride!

by Martin Rogowski
illustrated by Meryl Henderson

Jan and Ike like to **play**.
They can ride a bike.
Yes, Jan and Ike are quick.

Nine ride up, up, up.
Nine ride up the lane.
Jan can ride up.

Jan and Ike ride on.
Jan led Ike.
Jan gave Rex a quick nod.

The side lane is safe.
Jan and Ike ride in line.

Jan and Ike ride, ride, ride.
Can Ike get a quick time?
Can Jan win it?

Jan **has** a quick, quick time!
Ike did not quite win.
Jan and Ike had a fine ride!

# Unit 9



Word Count: 72

### Decodable Words

**Target Phonics Elements:** Blends *br, cr, dr, gr, tr*
*Bret, crack, drop, drum, grab, Greg, grin, trip*
**Review:** *at, big, bus, but, club, fun, hit, it, not, rim, six, step, tap, top, up*

### High-Frequency Words

*have, here, this, want*
**Review:** *a, and, do, the, to, you*



Word Count: 100

### Decodable Words

**Target Phonics Element:** Long *a* (*a_e*)
*cave, game, gaze, Jane, Kate, late, made, make, safe, wake*
**Review:** *big, box, can, dig, fun, had, hop, in, it, nap, not, on, run, sun, tan, up, yes, yet*

### High-Frequency Words

*help, too*
**Review:** *a, and, is, see, the, they*

## Week 3 • *Get Set! Ride!* ............... page 17

Word Count: 93

### Decodable Words

**Target Phonics Element:** Long *i* (*i_e*)
*bike, fine, lke, lane, like, line, nine, quite, ride, side, time*
**Review:** *can, gave, get, had, in, it, Jan, lane, led, nod, not, on, quick, Rex, safe, set, up, win, yes*

### High-Frequency Words

*has, play*
**Review:** *a, and, are, is, the, they, to*

**Decoding skills taught to date:**

Consonants /m/*m*, /s/*s*, /p/*p*, /t/*t*; Short *a*; Short *i*; Initial and Final /n/*n*; Initial /k/*c*; Short *o*; Initial and Final /d/*d*; Consonant /h/*h*; Short *e*; Blends *sn, sp, st*; Consonants /f/*f*, /r/*r*; Initial and Final /b/*b*; Consonant /l/*l*; Initial /k/*k*; Digraph *ck*; Short *u*; Initial and Final /g/*g*; Consonant /w/*w*; Consonants /ks/*x*, /v/*v*; Consonants /j/*j*, /qu/*qu*; Consonants /y/*y*, /z/*z*; Long *a* (*a_e*); Long *i* (*i_e*)